ALL

Hearts

Break the Same

LANCE T. LAMBERT

Fulton Books, Inc.
Meadville, PA

Published by Fulton Books 2020

ISBN 978-1-64654-790-6 (paperback)
ISBN 978-1-64654-791-3 (digital)

Printed in the United States of America

Hello, Beautiful People!

All of us will suffer heartbreak in our lifetimes. Most of us will suffer from it during our teenage years. Heartbreak comes in many different forms from many different people, and with heartbreak comes emotions that we've never felt before. Oftentimes, the strong emotions felt by our teenagers are dismissed due to the perception many of our adults hold about the fragility of adolescent minds. This book says no more. Your feelings are real and they are special. You deserve to be heard.

I hope this book offers some help to those struggling with their demons. You are not alone in this great, big world. You are strong. Again, you are special.

Some of you may cry.

Some of you may understand.

Some of you will choose not to comprehend the words in this collection.

All are okay.

I hope you enjoy it.

Peace, Love, Happiness

April 13, 2018

Reality isn't so real anymore. Whom to listen to, whom to follow, whom to love? All of these questions stand in front of me unanswered. I'm seventeen, I'm lonely, and I'm lost. With my whole future ahead of me, it seems as though my past refuses to let go. Whom do I trust? More importantly, whom do I love? That is, if I ever find the strength to love again.

Feel to Defy

I feel to defy,
defy Father, who told me that emotion was not part of masculinity,
that being a nice person meant I was weak.
He taught me that the overportrayal of confidence
meant I was strong enough to have a woman
and the tears that ran down my face during the
long nights of age seventeen meant I was not
ready to be eighteen.
It's as if being a man is a club only members are allowed into,
and only if you stay true to the values everyone else holds.
News flash:
this is no popularity fraternity.
It's an institution half of the population is born
into with no corporate box to fit.
We are humans of all emotions
and some may feel more than others,
that does not make them less of a man
rather, more human.
Less drown out by society
more intact with the heart.
I challenge all to feel
even when society tells us not to.

A Man

A man…
a man I always wanted to be
but when I told Father about my depression at fifteen
he proceeded to call me a pussy.
A man…
a man I always wanted to be
but the poetry I wrote was always too feminine.
I needed football and cars so people would
approve of my masculinity.
A man…
a man I always wanted to be
but when people listened to the wrong girl in high
school, that label was stolen from me.
I've been labeled as a boy my whole life
like some Peter Pan reincarnation here to never grow up.
I never liked hunting,
I never liked cars,
I still don't like going out to bars
but depression is real, and so is poetry,
and f—— that girl in high school who said those things about me
because I was a boy then, but I was a man to be.
So for the teenage boy lying in his bed restless as the night drags on
with tears in your eyes, thinking you're not good enough
looking for help but there's no one to turn to
because you're afraid of being "weak,"
I stand before you to tell you that those tears are okay

in this world you must stay
because you are a man, and I am too.
Just because we're not macho doesn't mean we can't be dudes.
We kid around, we care too much
but we're the ones who are always there when
everyone else's life is fucked up.
Society may deem us Peter Pan,
but most manly men could never save Neverland.
Stay true to yourself because you are amazing
and next time you're called a boy, make a stand
because you have and always will be a man.

You Didn't Tell Me

They told me that there weren't any monsters under my bed.
What they didn't tell me was, there would be ones in my head.
There would be times that I wouldn't have to
worry about what was under my bed
because my feet wouldn't make it to the ground that day.
They warned me about lying, cheating, stealing.
They warned me about knowing.
Knowing was too dangerous for creatures like us
but I was curious
so I tried sadness,
I tried death,
and I tried heartbreak.
Heartbreak.
Now I really know why they told me I shouldn't know
because it was worse than death.
I'm starting to think that the monsters were really never on the floor
they were waiting for me behind the door,
disguised as a brown-haired beauty
who could win me over with just one smile.
Yeah, maybe the rules don't really matter
and knowing does,
because whoever didn't warn us about
heartbreak was trying to protect us.
In the end, they, too, destroyed us.
Your heart cracks, then breaks, then falls apart.
Your body isn't yours anymore,

you hurt so deep inside your core,
you cry
until your tears dry.
You hurt until you don't feel.
It's the worst thing I have ever experienced and
I never saw it coming.
I was always worried about the monsters under my bed.

Teenage Trauma

It all hits you at once,
so overwhelming it feels as though it hasn't happened yet,
I saw it coming,
I couldn't prepare.
There's a disconnect between my brain and my heart
the wires run between the two, but they still
can't speak in their chemical language
so I go numb.
When the tears finally make their way to my eyes,
I don't sob.
I calmly sit in my own silence,
staring into the deep darkness of space that is now
blurry from the tears rushing down my face.
Did this really happen?
It doesn't seem real,
even though I saw it coming.
Never in a million years did I feel that we
would have this conversation,
like a mother birthing a child,
it doesn't seem like we should ever be separated.
We were one person.
Now I have to look for a fresh start,
am I born again?
Or is this what dying is like?
Here I am dealing with this adolescent melodrama,
welcome to my teenage trauma.

Don't Be Afraid to Cry

When I was three years old, I fell and scraped my knee,
my mother told me to man up,
nothing can hurt me physically.
I was eight and on the football field,
crying because I was scared, but my father told me to man up,
nothing can hurt me mentally.
At fifteen, my heart was broken for the first time
all alone in my room, crying by myself, and through the whimpers,
I cried, "Man up!"
Nothing can hurt me emotionally.
Maybe that's why I'm afraid to cry,
because society doesn't just tell us it's not okay,
they threaten to take our masculinity away.
If I cry, I'll no longer be human one day.
Just a sad sack of useless space, too emotional for his own good.
So I put on this mask and I raise my hood
because I wouldn't want anyone to think I was weak
and it doesn't just hurt me it hurts others too.
My own fear has me struggling to communicate with you
and I hate myself for it,
what am I supposed to do?
I've been brought up this way by the masses,
shamed for crying for my mother in my kindergarten classes.
I am incapable of saying how I feel instead,
I push my emotions deep down inside and I never heal.
I'm afraid to cry

and I'll end up pushing you away, saying goodbye
but I guess there's a reason why I'm here.
Take my advice,
I'm a man who wishes he would have cried as much as he wanted to
but was too afraid of what his friends would do
if they ever saw him like that.
I tuck it away and let my emotions walk
all over me like a welcome mat.
Now I've ended up in this dark place
but still no one sees my true face.
Go ahead, let those beautiful tears run down your cheeks
because that's what makes you human.
Your insides feel because you aren't bare,
sometimes your heart has to hurt so that you know it's still there.
Don't be afraid to set yourself free with the
tears of your transcendent soul
because after you lose a part of you,
you strangely become full.

Different

Of course, I'm different
I'm eighteen,
I like to read and write
I feel that love always wins,
I don't like to fight.
Yes, I play football but I'd rather spend my time in a book,
I just do these things when no one can look, this way
I fit in.
Fit in to this idea that I am the all-American
boy who does everything right
because ever since a young age, I was put into
the category of a Goody Two-shoes
I was the example used in class and pegged as a
winner, it seemed as though I couldn't lose,
yet that unneeded pressure on that nine-year-
old boy is why at eighteen I sing the blues.
Of course, I'm f—— different,
I'm the boy who doesn't speak
but when I put pen to paper, I find words with ease.
They reach me as if they were there the whole time.
'Cause instead of the weird silent kid
I could be the relatable fun one
but that name was never bestowed upon me.
The words never found my vocal chords in spite of me,
Of course, I'm different.
I love to be in a relationship, but I'm happiest when alone

it seems as though my happiest comes from within
but no one seems to understand.
Lonely and exhausted because I can't find the queen to my throne.
Of course, I'm different.
I'm the weird one, the castaway,
hoping to wake up and not be me one day.

Not Good Enough

The worst feeling I've ever felt,
watching you walk away with no traces to be left.
My mother warned me this day would come
but I didn't realize it would be this emotionally devastating.
Today is the day I realize
I'm not good enough...

I know I messed up
I lied, made you cry,
you threatened for me to be the reason for your death.
I also loved,
loved you more than myself,
greater than anyone ever could.

You were my life,
the reason why I took the next breath,
the reason I walked,
the only person to which I truly talked.
I loved, but now I'm lost
never thought it'd be this grounding
not being good enough.

The next guy's better than me,
I know because you told me,
but will he really ever see?
See you like I do?

You're my better half,
he doesn't get you like I do,
no one ever will.
I know people say this arbitrarily,
but has anyone else dedicated their heart on the page for you?
No matter how much effort I show
you don't notice.
This is the most devastating realization of life...
I'm not good enough.

May 1, 2018

    How silly was I to think that in a world full of shallow people, love would not be the same?

Alone in the Dark

I think we're alone now,
I look around and listen, but there's not a sound.
The only thing that fills my ears is the pound
of my own heart because you were supposed to
be home at dusk, and it's now after dark.

It's so hard to say goodbye, so when I drop you off,
I'll look right into your father's eyes and
I won't apologize for keeping you late;
there's nothing to apologize for.
As I sit here now looking at your beauty, I
wonder if I should make a mark.

Not on your body but on your soul.
The mark that would bring us together for an eternity
brings us into the age old fraternity.
They say we're too young, but I can feel this spark.

I know you do, too, as we sit here together,
the tension in the air,
I just can't help myself, if our love was a sentence,
there would be no question mark.

I move my lips towards yours and we meet.
How luscious they are to make a healthy boy, weak.
So wondrous, full of the most inspiring touch.
Another night like this will never exist—the sky,
the stars, surrounded by the romantic dark

As I kiss you, I work the courage up to reach for your heart
I hope you allow me to take it,
I'll let you grab mine.
We can join them together here under the sky of god's Arc.

The Other Woman

The other woman wasn't really a woman at all.
Yeah, I've kissed her before
and she held me while I cried myself to sleep a few times.
See, she's been there for me since my birthday
I mean, what else do I have to say?
At the time, I was trying to make you both happy,
but that wasn't good enough for either of you.
What should've been one option for me suddenly turned into two
I could choose her and stay,
or choose you and start over,
a fresh start with a hopeful view.
I was so young… I was so confused.
It should have never been a competition, yet
suddenly, it became a war of attrition.
The worst part is that I loved both of you and still do
but every time I saw either of the two, it was like a f—— audition
both of you seeing if I loved you more,
bidding for my favor like I was some street whore.
What for?
Now look at us…
I guess the other woman won,
but I'm not sure if that's true because what
she won was a shattered son.
The light gone from his world because he told his love he was done,

and now your light shines brighter than ever,
brighter than a thousand suns.
So even though it felt like you lost, I promise you,
you won.

Everything I'll Never Have

You're everything I've ever wanted.
You're everything I'd ever need.
You're my angel sent from above,
my heart, my one and only.
I had you,
better yet, I sustained you.
Now I'm missing you because I was too young and stupid
to realize how much I love you.
You're the best thing I ever had,
no one could compare,
but now I'm left sitting across the room
and all I can do is stare.
Stare at how your beauty lights the room like
the North Star lights the night sky,
and your laugh turns heads because it's so contagious
it attracts even the most cynical person
around you.
So stupidly in love with you,
and this time I'm mature enough to know it's true.
It's too late,
you're everything I've ever wanted and
everything I'll never have again.

Just Another Memory

I can't win this fight,
my mind, relentless,
fighting this opponent I can't see.
He's not here but he's everywhere, how can that be?
I need help,
I dropped the girl I love and now I pay heartbreak's fee.
No matter how much I try to hate her,
how mean she was to me,
I can't help but love her with all my heart.
Death is the only thing that should do us apart.
I already had several chances,
I wouldn't know where to start, so I start my
endeavor into an eternal darkness.
I love her.
my heart is sore,
the pain unbearable.
I'm lost without you
like a puppy without a collar, a businessman without a dollar.
It's not my fault that every time I see you my heart soars.
I tried so hard, yet
that might've been the problem.
I used all my energy quickly, then I ran out of options.
I realize we were different people when we were fifteen,
just two kids in love and nothing to see
but that kid still lives within me.
I can still see you on that second date.

On the dock, fishing.
Right about now you'd take the chance to tell me it
wasn't our second, date even though I count it
that way.
I'd argue right back, but somehow you always
found out how to get your way.
Maybe it was your pretty face
or those beautiful brown eyes.
Maybe it was that smile, the one I haven't seen in a while,
but I guess that's fair because I did this to myself.
I guess I'll just have to settle to be another memory on your shelf.

Two Is Better than One

They say two is better than one.
I had two once,
but then two left, leaving me with less than one.
Two didn't just leave with two's things;
two left with all the memories and love that two is associated with.
So I ask, is two worth the risk of being less than one?
Less than one is not a whole
just look at one's heart
there's an enormous f—— hole
and one is on the ground crying,
Looking at oneself, "Why, why, whying?"
One didn't understand the implications of being two
and one still doesn't understand how the other
one became more without one.
It's simple subtraction, two is less than one, but somehow two won.
Two found another one to become two again
and I guess that answers the question.
Once you find two again, you must win
because she's happy and I'm not.
In this depth of darkness and demons I rot.
It has to be because I don't have a two
but will I ever find a love that is true?
After all, I am less than one,
which means I need more than one to be two
but where do I find this more than one, and
if I do, does she even like me?

I don't think so because loving again is
like getting a blind man to see.
So I guess two is better than one
as long as two stays happy and believes they've won.

Empower(men)t

You leave holes in the conversation,
waiting for me to follow your crumb trail and fill them in
but there's a catch.
There are such things as right and wrong answers.
There's tricks and traps
and if I hit one, I have to watch you snap.
Punish me for guessing wrong
like I'm a prisoner and you already know
what answers you're looking for.
Like those black kids from Brooklyn,
The Central Park Five,
the white man calls them a prisoner of society
because of the color of their skin
fighting an uphill battle
but they can't win.
They never could.
Now my young teenage self is a prisoner,
a prisoner of a concept
a misconception of what was supposed to be empowering
has now been used to disempower me.
Independent, sure,
don't need no man…you're right,
but there's a difference between a b——— and a wife.
Unfortunately, most could go without knowing their whole lives.

Locked Up

What do you want from me?
I'll give you anything.
Loving you isn't enough,
hating you is too "immature" for your taste.
What do you want from me?
You can lock me up,
throw away the key,
or you can let me out,
but I know you'll never let me free.
For you, it's too easy.
Keep me caged up like a bird you own
but you can't stop me from singing,
I will cry out!
Cry out until someone hears me
and they'll open the door and let me be.
Right now you may see a bird that can't fly
but I know it takes time
and someone will come along,
turning this wingless bird into a soaring beauty.
What do you want from me?
I'm done waiting on love that isn't real
I need to know what it is you truly feel,
because I don't know right from wrong
all I know is how to sing my song.
I sit here waiting on a time
where I can love without your judgments cast upon mine.

A Text to the Next One

Right now you're in a state where you
think being independent is cool.
You think a man is someone who doesn't need a
woman and you can do anything by yourself.
You think that and what makes it worse is
that your friends think the same,
so behind the curtains, you make her
believe she's everything to you...
and she might actually be,
but she won't ever feel that way until you
make her the star of your show.
See, she likes to come off as more complicated than she really is,
and you might actually think she's kind of complicated sometimes,
but she's as simple as it gets.
She's the happiest person on this planet,
the only job you have is keeping the permanent
smile she holds on her face.
Don't be fifteen-, sixteen-,seventeen-year-old me,
don't take things for granted,
don't value anyone else over her,
and most importantly, don't try too hard,
and what I mean by that is, don't worry
about what anyone else thinks.
Your friends, your family, your anybody, their
opinions go out the f—— window

because the greatest tragedy in your life will be
when you let others fog your mental up and
you end up losing the girl of your dreams for good
because she doesn't come around often.
She's beautiful from head to toe,
the nicest, kindest soul anyone's ever met,
and she has a genuine loyalty and love for anyone
who has the blessing to be in her circle,
especially for her significant other,
so don't be the immature, insecure fifteen-year-old
who thought he had something to prove because
you have nothing to prove.
You've already proven everything by being in a relationship with her,
all you have to do is hang on,
so feed her; trust me, she says she's not hungry but
she really is… Buffalo chicken dip is her
favorite.
Listen to her, don't come up with replies while
she's talking, truly understand her,
she loves to rant, so just sit back and enjoy her facial
expressions, I swear she lights up the room
without even knowing it.
The funniest one to me is when she scrunches her
nose when she's frustrated with something. It'll
make you want to smile, but don't do that; she won't like that.
Compliments, compliments, compliments—
start everyday by telling her she's pretty and go
to bed with something of the same.
She's drop-dead gorgeous but sometimes she forgets.
Support her.
Again, she's one of a kind. She can literally do anything
she puts her mind to. Let her know that.

Also, she's independent, as can be so; even if you
don't want her doing it, she's going to do it.
Just support her.
There's a lot more advice I could give, but most
importantly, just please, dear god, take care of her.
Like, even if you don't do anything else, just love her.
She's a tough independent girl but she loves
to be taken care of. Even when there's nothing wrong,
take some time to hold her, play with her
hair, rub her back.
When she's sick,
force her to take her medicine because if not, she's
going to forget on purpose. Put Netflix on
and rub her back while you're forced to watch Grey's
Anatomy. I know it's not the most pleasant thing in
the world, but she loves it, so do it for her and enjoy it for her.
The grossest one is when she has trouble pooping.
You're going to have to sit there and rub her back
while you listen to her s——. And you'll think
to yourself, how is something so disgusting coming
out of a human this beautiful? But you'll do
it because she needs you to.
When she's drunk,
she's a f—— goofball! She's going to act crazy and
sometimes flirty, and that might piss you
off, but it's harmless.
Trust me, in two seconds, when you make eye contact,
she'll jump on you and start making out
with you like no one is watching.
And at the end of the night (the end of the night
might be earlier than you think), hold her hair
back while she throws up.

Then hold her up, take her hair out, wash her face,
brush her teeth, take her clothes off for her,
and put her to bed.
Sit there holding her while she snores and
appreciate how beautiful she is.
Because she loves you.
And the next morning, make her breakfast just for
the fact that you had a ton of fun with her last
night.
She's amazing.
Don't miss your chance.
Because I sure did...

To Your Future Lover

Yes, it's true,
I failed miserably.
I guess it's a valid question if you should actually be listening to me.
Yes, it's true,
I called her names and at times just didn't feel the same.
Yes, it's true,
I loved her with all my heart and treated
her like a prized piece of art.
Yes, it's true,
I still love her, and so I write this letter to her future lover.

It wasn't that we didn't get along but that I was too young,
so I pass the torch in hopes that someone can
make her happier than I ever did.
Treat her right and never allow the love to go arid
because there will come a time when things get pretty rough.
Every ship sees a near fatal storm,
but in those times, I hope you keep her warm.

She's an independent gal;
if you try to tell her no, she'll do it anyhow,
but no matter how tough she likes to act,
there will come a time where she's nothing but cracked.

In these times, I hope you're a better man than
my teenage self ever hoped to be,

'cause if not, then she's gonna leave.
Then you'll be stuck in this hell just like me,
burning emotionally for an eternity.

Hold her until she falls asleep,
look into those brown eyes and how they go so deep
and just f—— love her.
That is what she deserves and the reason we aren't together.

Yes, it's true, I love that girl more than I love myself.
It's also true that I was too immature to handle a love that strong.
I was a scared, confused teenager and I did her wrong;
now I must watch from afar, like the stalker she
thought she had, in the tree outside of the
bedroom window.

Yes, it's true, I lost the love of my life,
I thought one day she'd be my wife,
but she's yours now, and this has come into public view.
Please, whatever you do,
treat her right.

Heart on Love

I listened to my Heart,
then he broke himself.
I caught him one day playing with a belt,
tying it around his neck until he turned purple.
I ran to him,
kept him from bursting.
I sat with him for some time
crying, cursing.
The bruises running down his body made him weak.
They'll heal but they won't ever leave.
I asked him why he would do this to himself,
he said Love…
Love did this to him;
love was a she who liked the same things as he.
She earned his trust that he valued so much
and sucked him in
then left him, leaving him begging in the end.
Heart said Love meant the world
such a special, special girl.
Love had a certain way about her.
Love made Heart feel alive,
more alive than any feeling ever could,
took him places no drug would,
but then Love left Heart to die,
left him conflicted.
Love left Heart when he was still addicted.

The withdrawals grew harder and harder,
Heart diminishing into nothing more than a
loaf of bread left in the back of the box,
just waiting to eat himself alive.
Love went on and found herself a new heart,
while Heart was stuck in me.
Love can flee,
but Heart has to stay indefinitely.
And that
was the toughest love story anyone has ever told me.

May 20, 2018

I'm seventeen, my grad party was yesterday, and then I proceeded to go out with my friends. The whole squad was there, and lemme tell ya, it was the time of our lives. I had a great time with my friends, hooked up with a random chick, and ended up pulling the trigger before passing out.

Drunk Depression

I'm lying here in a room full of darkness,
thinking about how much I f—— hate this.
Why did I do this to myself?
It all comes rushing to my heart when I'm by myself
and I've tried to put all the memories in the depths of my boxes
but I keep bringing them out like a child attached to his favorite toy.
If only at the time I wasn't such a boy.
I'm drowning in darkness, in tears, in beer
and I don't know what to do like a helpless baby deer,
limping around the woods, wounded in the worst place of all.
I'm in a place called the twilight zone, an eternal fall
and I can't even think about life without you.
You were once my everything,
I couldn't see past you.
I don't want to be here anymore.
Saying your name hurts me deep in my soul,
I'm crying so much that my eyes are sore.
I love you and I hate me.
I know I've exhausted all my chances,
nothing in this life comes for free.
So I sit here drowning in darkness, in tears, mostly in beer,
because when I can't remember that I cried
it's like it never happened at all
and this keeps me from picking the phone up to call

May 21st, 2018

    I sit here alone in the dark as my head throbs. I should've worked out today but I got too fucked up. I made out with two more girls last night, so that makes three this weekend. I'm finally letting myself go.

In the Back of a Car Full of Teenagers

I'm OKAY
I'm OKAy
I'm OKay
I'm Okay
I'm okay.
Stay strong.
Please stay strong.
The first tear hits the floor,
I'm not okay.
None of you can see,
but I'm crying for help silently.
Please…
Help me.

Tough

They say, "Dry it up…quit being weak."
They say, "Do you want me to give you a real reason?"
They say, "You're soft. Everyone goes through that."
It's not weak,
it's not soft,
not at all.
In fact, letting a tear roll softly down my cheek,
letting it fall in front of someone I care deeply about
is one of the toughest things I've ever done.

Every Night

Every night I have to see you.
I tell myself to clear my mind,
but you
I can always find.
It's been a long time since I've called you mine,
but my heart likes to bring you up in conversation,
you have no clue,
I still love you,
I really do.
Every night in my dreams
I love you, I kiss you, I hug you
I give you all the attention you want and I never say no.
I wasn't the best boyfriend, I know.
I replay the worst situations and make them the best.
The parts that tore us apart are now the ones that bring us together,
but you know none of that
because it isn't real.
My eyes are closed, and I'm the only one who can see,
the boyfriend I could be is all just a dream

Guardian Angel?

It's a dream that keeps coming back,
not every night,
but when it does come, I'm sure to remember it when I wake up.

I'm driving on a road,
it seems so familiar, but I can't quite say where I am.
I'm driving with someone,
the tall, shadowed man seems friendly, but he doesn't speak.
He smiles a bright smile that blinds me with
the power of a thousand suns,
I snap my head back and focus on the road.

It seems as though we are heading to a
place I should be excited about,
but my steering wheel isn't steady.
I'm having trouble keeping us on the road,
light poles pass us by rapidly, and suddenly there's a million
I couldn't miss them if I tried.
They're blinding me,
my steering wheel keeps pointing towards them and I lose it.

But my friend is there,
keeping us straight.
I ask him, "Why?"
But I get no reply,
I wake up.

May 28, 2018

Hungover? Yes. Had fun last night? Yes. Possibly struggling with depression? Maybe. I have a great life. I'm a happy kid 99% of the time, but sometimes I get into a lull where I get down on myself and I can't seem to get up. It's like I'm so overwhelmed I can't fight it and it swallows me up. I don't know what to do about it. I can't talk to anyone. I'm the happy-go-lucky, golden child. Life's not tough for me. I just don't understand why I feel the way I do.

May 29, 2018

    I woke up at 10:00 a.m. today with the worst hangover ever. Grad week has been fun but now I need to slow down. On the other hand, I miss her. I know she's not good for me, but she's an amazing person. Yes, I do love her. I guess I just miss her presence and need to see her again. It doesn't help that I'm down in the dumps as well.

Shooting Stars

As I sit here next to you, looking at the moon and the stars,
I can't help but compare them to you.
How their lights just don't shine the same way your smile does,
the love being made under them tonight doesn't
compare to the love you have in your heart,
and the dreams being wished for when they shoot
don't compare to the dreams that you make
come true.
I can't believe I'm doing this right now,
but just like when the sun comes up, I have to say goodbye to them,
I'm saying goodbye to you too.
Lately I've failed to let you shine, leaving you blue.
I can't be who you want me to,
I try to keep up to the star you are, but I'm the
moon in the background stealing from you.
I'm not mad at you, I'm mad at myself
for having an ego that couldn't succumb to yours.
Now I'm stuck crashing with these wild whores
back again as a stallion, a wild horse,
because I could never be the trained Clydesdale you wanted of me.
You're the star of your own show now,
shooting across the night, lighting up the sky.
Let me ask you this:
have you ever seen two shooting stars shoot at the same time?

May 30, 2018

    To whoever is reading this, keep grinding. I believe in you.

#PeaceLoveHappiness

This Is What You Do to Me

I walked into the red front door of my overprotective
home this morning, and my mother knew I
had seen you.
It's the look that people get when they see a ghost
or when hearing a gunshot not too far away.
Mouth open,
dark circles around the eyes,
painted black from the weary battle I had with my mind,
walking slowly but heavily as if my mind
was weighing my body down.
My shoulders and knees weak from the fight I've been through,
I have no one else to blame but myself.
No matter how many times is the last time,
I always say, "Well, maybe one more."
You're a repressed thought that I keep bringing to the forefront.
I can't look away,
I walked in this morning and went straight to bed,
trying to escape the emotional combat,
my heart fights with my head.
It's a tragedy that a young man could be so scared of his youth,
especially with so much in front of him.
But I have to look back
because this is what you do to me.

Those Deep Brown Eyes

Those deep brown eyes,
the ones I could stare into and get lost in for days,
capturing me and my heart simultaneously for years.
Just one flash,
one look and
I was lost like a baby seeing the world for the first time.
Those deep, deep brown eyes,
I could connect my heart to yours through
those beautiful brown eyes.
Our souls coming together to create a
perfect unity between two lovers,
I never thought I could see another pair of eyes that perfect.
Those deep, deep, deep brown eyes.
My dad always told me that eyes tell lies, but yours
were too pure to ever do such a thing,
and when I see them now, I'm still lost like
that fifteen-year-old kid was,
but I guess it's a different lost now.
Those years never turned into a lifetime
like I wished they could have,
and those eyes have a different meaning because
they look at someone else now,
every now and then, they might look at me,
but it's usually through a screen,
and it's not the same message that I used to get when I was a teen.
I was lost and immature, and

those eyes kept looking at me,
I finally saw their suffering,
the look of pure defeat when your eyes didn't
seem so full of hope anymore.
This is all I have left, an apology to those deep brown eyes
because when I left, I didn't see the only
light in the world at the time,
and when I said goodbye to those deep, brown eyes,
I shut them for good, leaving myself in a world of darkness.
Those deep, deep, deep, deep brown eyes,
I love you.

Late Night

Deeper and deeper into the night,
harder and harder to see the light.
It consumes me.
My mind labors all day,
but I still can't sleep at night.
These tireless thoughts consume my being,
they're hungry and they don't stop feeding.
I'm in an endless tunnel, I have a hard time seeing,
I close my eyes and I can finally see them.

Depression to my left,
Anxiety to the right,
All of my regrets stand in front.
I wonder why my mind is so hard to confront.

It tells me to get better,
turns around and tells me to dismiss these thoughts.
It's a contradicting cycle, spinning me into the ground.
I'm a rocket man but I'm downward bound,
heading to a place with no stars in the sky
and dreams only go to die.
I'm lost and I will be forgotten.
I've neglected myself, and my mind has rotten.
I open my eyes.

I can't see them, but they're still there,
circling, haunting me through the air,
my mind runs all day,
but I get no sleep.
My thoughts consume me, and I'm afraid I'm too deep.

June 2, 2018

The depression comes and goes now. Usually it just comes around at night.

Not the Right Time

Then you told me it wasn't the right time.
The time may come somewhere in the future.
Leaving me wandering aimlessly, waiting on
a ghost that refuses to haunt me.

Endless Track

I've lost track of the days,
the hours,
the minutes,
the seconds.
They all run together in an endless loop.
My mind keeps dancing,
but the same song plays over and over.
It never stops,
I want to turn it off but
I don't know how.
I'm trapped in my own head,
every door I open leads to nothing,
no way out.
Surrounded by endless darkness in a world full of light,
like a plant that never sees the sun in its life,
I continue to wither
until I'm so frail I can't depend on myself.
I hate me.
I'm so weak
my bed is the only place that feels safe.
So pale,
so bleak,
covered with dried tears.

In my head for over a month,
but it feels like it's been years.
Everything runs together,
I lose track,
I just want my mind back.

To Gracie

―――――――――――――――――― ⁕ ―――――――――――――――――――

Graceon, I love you.
I love you, even though you were never created,
and that's unfortunate, but your mom and I just never made it.
You were my first baby girl,
you were my whole world.
Just because your mom and I could not see our future clearly
doesn't mean you're any less real to me.
Graceon, I love you,
which means I must I apologize—
apologize for not being the man your mother needed me to be.
I was a lost boy, a sailor with no ship at sea,
drowning in my own insecurities.
I apologize to you
for not being able to be your dad because
I forgot about you and me,
and I must give my love to another daughter of mine.
I must be the shoulder that holds her head while she's crying
and I must be the source of that smile,
the smile that's half mine and half her mother's.
I just wish I could've seen your smile.
That would have made my life worthwhile.
Your dark bouncing curls and your deep blue eyes,
I can see them now.
A spitting image of your mother you would've
been, but I threw in the towel.
I apologize to you.

Please find it within yourself to forgive me.
I was an insecure little boy whose life was about to be destroyed,
and even though I'll never hold you,
my love for you will always be true.
So please forgive me, beautiful,
because my idea of you is truly wonderful.
Graceon, I love you.

Heart Play

I came back and you denied me.
I tried,
tried,
tried.
Your manner still managed to change.
I saw your eyes lighten up, like you heard something strange.
Something changed in that beautiful little mind of yours,
something that made you forget all those years…
the years of suffering I put you through.
Oh, I can't say how sorry I am for producing so many of your tears,
without you I'm nothing.
I love you and I'm now old enough, I realize
and as I'm smooth talking, I can see you
fighting a battle on the inside.
Your heart says no, but ours say yes.
you flash your eyes at me and roll them,
and just like that,
I know I've won this game of chess.
You say yes to breakfast because that's your favorite,
I've gotten another chance and I get overly excited,
but then something happens and we don't go.
My mind shifts,
my heart dies.

I open my eyes, expecting you to be there to say hello,
but there's nothing there.
Just another instance of happiness when my
mind sends my heart out to play.

Just Feel

It's okay to hurt.
Apologize for nothing.
Feel it in your soul.

Lonely Dreamer

I'm not really a get-up go-getter
and always-ready-to-go partier.
I'm more of a brooding, full-hearted sleeper,
the guy who hides his emotions but will tell you, "I love ya."
I like to lie in bed all day and listen to Metallica.
The best smell in the world are fresh dryer
sheets that come out of the box,
and the best sight is when the clouds meet the night
sky, drawing a line between city and god.
It's beautiful, even though I know those clouds are man-made,
but my imagination tells me there's something
mysterious about the moonlight hitting daylight
objects.
I'm not quite sure what it is;
I guess I'm a hopeless romantic.
Wander fascinates me.
I think I'm a little different,
I'm silent, even though I have a lot to say,
and I enjoy lying down perpendicular to a wall,
having my legs straight up against it as if my
feet belong with those clouds in the sky.
I wish I could touch it,
the sky.
I guess I'm more of a lonely dreamer,
a misunderstood, caring lover.

Keep It In

People ask, "Why does your writing seem so sad?"
I haven't thought about it.
There just comes a time when the happy child must break,
when you keep every sad moment in,
in an attempt to keep that ever-so-special smile on your face.
The emotion has to go somewhere.

I'm the protector,
the happy kid with a golden smile to offer.
My people confess their sad thoughts to me like
a devout Christian confesses his sins,
but I'm no man of god.
There's no one to turn to when I can't keep everything in.

It's not that I don't want this,
there's strength in always being the strong one,
beauty in having the shoulder that people cry on,
but sometimes when I'm alone
and the darkness slowly creeps in,
it's so hard
to keep it in.

I don't know what It is.
It chokes me up at night,
spins my head, overwhelming me until I can't fight.

It makes me so sad I cry until I don't have any sight,
like being caught in a rainstorm and your
windshield wipers don't wipe.

It is there,
all I know is, I have to keep It in,
but sometimes,
I don't know how.

June 14, 2018

I still get lonely without her sometimes.

Lone Star

As I look up to the cloudy darkness that is the night sky,
I ponder on a thought that has intrigued
me since being a young boy:
the North Star has to be lonely at night.
It may be surrounded by a few friendly stars, but none can compare,
the brightest burning,
most magical,
most potential-filled being in the universe,
it has to get lonely.
No one there to ask for help,
the insurmountable responsibility that others have put on her.
No one asking if she needs help,
but everyone asking if they could receive some.
She leads everyone in the right direction but has none herself.
She has to be lonely.

Mission Failed

I thought I could do it,
drink my whiskey until I heard the "la la
la" of the angels I've prayed to,
but all I did was gag vile all over myself until I
smelled like a bar restroom at 2:00 a.m.
My friends were there to make sure I didn't lie on my back,
and I couldn't make the words out to tell them to let me do it;
I want to go.
This existence is a miserable, shallow quest,
all I can do is lie in bed looking at her picture,
wishing for another chance.
My dreams don't escape her,
my eyes don't see past her.
What we had was special,
but I wasn't smart enough to keep her.
I'm not even smart enough to do it.
I close my eyes and don't open them,
a miserable existence that I can't escape,
nothing to do but try again.

June 20, 2018

Smoked weed for the first time last night and tripped so hard. It was like I had a dream inside of a dream inside of a dream.

Beautiful World

I find pink elephants chasing blue butterflies in the sky.
Trees flow against the wind,
and your body tells no lies.

Where god is in the eyes of her people
and the devil sees no justice for evil.
A place of legend.
Only one way to get there.

The ticket is grown,
grown tall so it can take you to the clouds.
Man took it away,
but the angels delivered it back.
We could find a place much better than this.

The place where baby's laughter fills the air
and water drops fall softly in your hair.
Worries melt like butter into a puddle of happiness,
and there are no demons, inner or outer.

It only takes a few steps to open the gate,
just hold, kiss, puff, blow, and wait.

Nothing

I don't know how I feel.
The best way to describe it is…
nothing.
I feel nothing.
Pain is nothing.
Love is nothing.
Hurt is nothing.
Happy is nothing.
I feel nothing.
An empty body knowing I should feel a thing but don't.

Everything flows through me like a quiet stream,
but no matter how much current, nothing feels anything.
Is my heart still beating?
I know I'm breathing,
but does that mean I'm still alive?
Am I just a lost soul trying to find the next body?
This one doesn't seem to be human.
I scratch, I hit, I claw, I cry,
but still…
Nothing.

Numb

Other girls fill the needs of my attraction,
but they don't give me satisfaction
because my heart was once broke, but I've patched it up,
and if I did it right,
everything would be looking up,
but I failed to forget about the human in me,
and instead of love, I've filled my heart with concrete.
I sit here, thinking of you and them,
feeling everything and nothing at the same time,
and I ask myself, am I empty?
Or am I just no longer the big-hearted
handsome young man I once was?
I know people change,
but do they lose their emotional range?
If I do lose my feeling, does that mean I am healing?
These questions circle my mind during the day,
spinning me into the ground no matter how hard
I fight,
and they turn into the monsters under
my bed that haunt me at night.
I don't recognize the heart that lies inside of me anymore.
I'd say it was dormant but I can still feel it beat like
little children running on the hardwood
floor. I can hear the laughter coming from the
children, but it's so distant I don't recognize it.
I'm as numb as a drunken sailor washed ashore.

I wish I could feel, but to feel is
to live,
and to live is to be
in pain.
I'd much rather sit here feeling nothing than
truly live.

June 22, 2018

When your mind says no, you need to say yes. I put myself through living hell, so I know when heaven comes.

Our Door

Momma told me to never give up my happiness,
but there came a time where it was either yours or mine,
and I knew after the temporary pain you'd be fine,
so I left the only love I ever knew.
It was right person wrong time,
I sit here in perpetual sadness during this write time,
silently weeping in this poem.
It's been a year, but I can't get over the fact you were once mine.
I've come to terms that I was your sacrifice.
My happiness for yours,
it's like I'm stuck in a dark room and there are no doors
because the only door that I have ever known
was the best door of them all.
I chose to shut it.
Shut it in your face and never look back,
at least,
never tell you that I would look back
because I know I can't.
If I did try to open that door again, I wouldn't be
able to find you because you found so many
other doors.
Much better doors with better faces,
better opportunities,
better hearts.
As I look at our door, I see a grand red door at the
head of a Southern plantation mansion.

When you look, you see the entrance to a mouse's home.
Just a small, meaningless point in the grand
scheme of the structure of your home,
but I know I have to settle for that little hole in the wall.
I wanted us to be the door I never had to shut,
but I proceeded to do just that.
Our door was everything I wanted and more.
Now our door is forgotten lore.

Mary Jane

I walk in and there's one girl I want to see.
I sit next to her, and she kisses me.
She's a beautiful girl, smoking hot.
When I'm with her, I'm worry free.

Her touch is as light as sunny day clouds,
her kiss as smooth as silk.
She touches me just right,
she's my escape on weekend nights.

She takes me to a special place,
A place I feel completely safe,
I love her.
I love everyone.
I never want our time together to be done.

She goes by Mary,
others call her Jane,
and she's as refreshing as a midsummer's rain.

Swallow Me

Swallowed by the darkness.
Such a tiny moment in such a big, big world.
Easily forgotten.
Stuck in time.
Lost forever,
no one seems to notice,
not even me.
I don't know how it happened,
I was so happy,
now my depression and anxiety swallow me.
My existence.
Inside the monster of depression,
down his throat,
in the belly of the beast,
in the darkness,
listen to the lost voices.
Mutters and murmurs of lives that once were lived,
lives that were never fulfilled.
People are born with light in their eyes.
I once had that light,
my angelic blue eyes have gone dim,
so has the skin under them.
Someone swallow the sadness,
the crippling depression,
the anxiety.
Please swallow me.

July 7, 2018

I get drunk and then cry. That's what I do. This way, when I wake up in the morning, I will feel the weight of the emotional distress that I've been through, but there will be no tears left to cry. For that, I am thankful because the tears you remember are the hardest to bear.

To My Future Self

It's really tough right now, and I'm not sure if I'm close to the end,
I'm surrounded by darkness and demons,
hoping, praying that I don't break, just bend.
Absolute hell,
it's not life but myself that I hate.
I look in the mirror, and what used to be a burning blaze
is now wet firewood, only capable of producing a pathetic haze.

There's still hope.
So when you read this, I wish you are doing well.
Holes through your identity you no longer poke
because you're better than that,
and even though I can't get myself to see that
right now, I know you'll know.
Healing takes time.
It's a lot like when you were little and broke your toe.
It hurts a lot when it first happens and it may
not heal as quickly as you want it to,
but eventually we got back to normal and
our foot fit back in our shoe.

Our heart is torn in half by a girl we loved with all we had,
but it's not her fault it's ours.
Our young self's thinking process was bad,
but I'm hoping eventually someone can
come along and fix it for me.

Someone that would lie in bed with me for hours,
someone who doesn't like tea
because it's disgusting.
Someone who understands that I'm hard to live with
and pounds my ass into shape when I need it like a blacksmith
because you and I both know sometimes we stray from the path,
and we really need someone else to bring us back.
I hope you find this girl
or maybe a different us will along the way.
I just hope it happens soon,
the clock keeps ticking day by day.

July 15, 2018

The drugs blurred my vision. I can't see you anymore.

Trapped

Surrounded.
Four white walls made of white brick in a white room.
They close in on me,
inching in on my body,
closer,
closer.
Lying on my back,
motionless,
helpless.
I look to the window for help,
it's gone.
The white room is now dark,
walls keep moving in.
I'm the only person in the room.
Everyone else,
hurt,
locked out,
pushed away.
What do I look like?
How do I feel?
Am I okay?
The walls start talking,
they know the truth,
the only friends that know me.

They trap me.
They set me free.
They isolate me.
They're all I need.

Addicted to Hurt

I let it penetrate my skin,
soaking in it like a bubble bath for within.
It crawls to my heart
like a quiet cougar creeping on its prey,
then builds its home right there.
I'd try to get better but I don't know where to start.
I'm sick, penetrated by a disease,
begging for mercy
asking god, please, please,
but there's no answer.
This is the life meant for me.
I love her.
So I sit here
surrounded by painfully happy memories.
The thought of her smile,
it's starting to grow.
I don't stop it, I let it soak.
Fill me up,
I crave it,
I love it.
Make me hurt,
this is what I deserve,
my mind eats itself alive
like a cannibal trying to survive.
She goes out,
she thrives.

I've taken a deep dive
and then went even further down.
Every time I think I'm out,
there's another person there to drown me back down.
The thing is,
I soak in it.
I'm addicted to it,
and it starts from within

My Sweet Escape

Real life is especially hard sometimes,
the minute details weighing on your brain,
high frequencies sitting right behind your forehead,
creating an excruciating pain.
We all need a break.
You were my escape, but like most pastimes,
I grew out of that phase.
The absence of you brought the absence of fun,
living without you made me numb,
worrying about the ticks and tocks that drive us nutty.
It's a miserable thing when you're running
from your past into the future.
There's no present.
Then I found her, and she took me places I couldn't see before,
she made me laugh until my stomach hurt,
made me play with no worries,
she brings me to the present and holds on tight,
making me feel warm and loved on the inside.
It's a new perspective—
one that makes life not so hard sometimes.

Our Song

Our song used to be the sweet song of a bluebird
peacefully resting in the treetop.
Our song used to be as refreshing as a gust of cool summer breeze.
Our song used to be as peaceful as sitting by a
creek bed in the night, watching the stars.
When we listened to our song, it would make time stop.

Our song has lost its way.
All of my days are filled with black and grays.
I sit here on this creek bed, but it's not night
I melt under the scorching sun, looking for that refreshing white,
but there's nothing left in me, there's no fight.
The bluebirds are now ravens, circling their prey,
and all I can do is pray.

Pray that I wasn't your prey
because our song has now been changed.
Every time I hear it, I feel estranged
and I guess that's what I am—
a sad sap who lost his to-be wife prematurely
because he was young and acted immaturely.

I listen to our song to this day, telling myself it was just a phase.
Every now and then I hear that bluebird
but I remind myself even a crow can disguise himself as a songbird.
Our song used to be the symbol of our life,
now it just means that I've eternally lost my wife.

Understanding My Mind

You say you don't understand me,
that I do and say things that don't make sense.
Try being me.

I wake up happy,
the rest of the day I'm sad.
I'm at peace one second,
the next I'm mad.

The day swirls around me constantly,
I tell myself I'm not the center, but the
world spins round and round
I'm walking high one minute but then feeling
I would be better off in the ground.

It's a beautiful mind, this one of mine,
I try to let it shine,
but it's not accepted.

Not even by me.
I keep to myself,
a wolf pretending to be a sheep.

I can't let them know about the true beast,
if they did, they wouldn't get it.
I'd be outcasted like a toy to the island of misfits.

Your Memory

Your memory will forever be on my mind.
Not just in the back drifting around with the
countless memories that I could find
but up front, on my mind every day because
that's how much you mean to me.
I've come to terms that this is how it's going to be,
forever basking in the essence of your memory.

I try to convince my heart that this is the way it was meant,
but no matter how hard I try, I stay hell-bent,
because a memory you can love,
but a memory you can't give a hug.
A memory stays young forever,
but the plan was to grow old together.
A memory doesn't get sick, and it doesn't need any attention,
but when I hear your name, I can feel the tension.

The tension that always reminds me that I let you down.
You deserve a prince that will take care of
you and treat you like the crown,
love you,
take you out on the town.

I wanted to do all of it but I didn't do any of it,
proving what everyone else was saying.
So here I am, just me and your memory,

doing this dance that leads me nowhere.
The hardest part wasn't the things I did or said,
but the ideas that bloomed and are now dead.

Addicted to Criticism

I enjoy looking at myself in the mirror,
I'm a different kind of narcissist,
a self-defeating, self-involved, hopeless soul who
enjoys picking apart the image before him.
My hair,
too long
my shoulders,
too broad
or maybe not broad enough?
My abs,
more like a cardboard box of Busch Light than the
ideal washboard I've wanted since I was a
pudgy three-year-old.
My face tells the story of a young man who has been
beaten down, built up, then beaten down
again.
It's an opposite narcissism,
more of an addiction to criticism.
I've been told I'm not good enough and I liked it.
It gave me things to work on in life,
making me feel like I could get better.
I didn't realize the things I was working on
weren't things that get better.
There was nothing to get better at when it came to me,
you just wanted me to be someone else.
Someone I couldn't be.

I convinced myself that the man for you was what I wanted,
so I liked it.
Soon you didn't have to tell me,
I was changing myself daily and
I still wasn't good enough.
Not being good enough for you wasn't good enough for me,
so the deconstructive criticism continued and carries on.
I look at myself and try to like what is in front of me,
but most days I give in to the twisted vision of what I see.

July 21, 2018

I wonder if I'll ever meet a girl able to deal with me.

July 21, 2018.

I hope so.

 Your Name

Your name
hurts my ears to hear, like the music we used
to listen to on late-night drives,
hurts my heart because it floods with all
the memories that come with it,
hurts my eyes because the mere sight of the
scribbles that spell your name bring pain.
Even though it hurts me to think about your name,
I cannot deny the fact that the sound of your
name was like songbirds on a bright sunny day.
Your name,
your name was supposed to be my name.
Your name used to make my heart leap right out of my chest,
but now my heart can do no leaping
because the sound of the syllables of your name
hitting someone's lips ties ropes on my heart
and doesn't allow it to jump for anything.
Your name,
a name I used to write on paper when I was bored
in class because the sight of it fulfilled me.
Your name isn't just your name,
it's a reminder of the bad times we had together,
of my faults and my failures,
but it's not the bad that hurts.
It's all the good.
Your name isn't just your name,

it's a representation of the goodness in my life,
the two years of love and happiness we spent together.
This is what makes my heart burn as I spend my
time scrolling through your Twitter feed.
Yes, your Twitter feed because it wasn't just your
looks; it was your mind that intrigued me so
heavily.
Your name isn't just your name,
your name brings me you.
I still love you.

August 31, 2018

I am awakening once again. Out of the depths of heartbreak I have risen. It's taken me some time, but I may have made it. I'm blessed.

Butterflies

Oh, that familiar feeling…how I've missed it.
The one where your mood matches mine,
and I look into your eyes,
all of a sudden, sparks fly.
That moment never fails to give me butterflies,
and now it's back
with someone new.
This feat only a few can do,
I didn't know anyone else could do it other than you.
This girl gives me butterflies,
and she doesn't come with lies,
strings tied,
or other guys.
Maybe her butterflies won't die.
They will continue to flourish and fly,
fly until both our wings meet
when we become one.

My New Fantasy

What's your greatest secret?
Do you think you can keep it?
I want to know your dreams and your desires.
You're not just another fad.

I can tell that you're special.
The way you carry yourself,
it's not superficial.
Nothing like I'm used to.

Go out with me?
That's if you want to.
The problem is, I don't know if you're real.
Is it my heart or my head that's not completely healed?

I can't tell,
I guess I'll sit back and admire you from afar.
You don't know it, but I wish for you like a shooting star.

No Control

For someone who struggles with it,
I enjoy losing control often.
Maybe that's the part of me I try to escape,
the part that holds on ever so tightly,
maneuvering,
manipulating,
trying to play god.
The drugs take me away,
with it, my responsibility that I owe to myself
to be the law-abiding poster boy I was taught to be.
They say it's bad for me,
but it teaches me to be carefree,
break the boxes they've put me in.
After all, it takes strength to go places you've never been.
I've never been to me.

I hate losing control.
Sober that is,
in real life control wins.
Control you.
Control me.
Control everything.
A race for power
and control reigns supreme.
I can't do it,
free will is too important, but no one seems to agree.

Just give me a couple hours
to be in a place I feel I belong.
Carefree,
no control,
no responsibility.

Here We Go Again

It passed my mind again today,
I thought I was done with it,
but what can I say?
Driving down the road,
thinking about one wrong turn.
My family could tell themselves it was an accident.
Those things happen, right?
Let's face it—
I don't have enough courage for that s——.
That...
now that would be one hell of a hit.
They would be devastated when I died too,
along with my brothers and sisters.
They'd blame it on themselves.
I know how they are,
I could never take them that far.
I've been deep into a hole,
so deep that I never thought I'd return to my soul.
I thought I was back,
I guess I was wrong.
I drift in and out of my body as if I inhabit two worlds,
crying in both,
like two little birds.
Would it actually hurt?
Maybe the body
but not the soul.
I thought it was done,
but it looks like another battle has just begun.

September 23, 2018

Her birthday. What I'd do to be able to tell her happy birthday, give her presents, and smother her in love. The happy birthday wouldn't mean much, and the presents would be small because I'm broke, but the love would be unlike any other. It would be my love—something that not a lot of people are capable of giving. She loved my love. Not in a sexual way but in an "I care about you" way. The hugs, the kisses, the way I held her—I miss all of it. But I messed it up. There's a void in my life. I have yet to get over her because my self-respect lies within her recognition of me.

January 5, 2019

I looked through my old phone, and that was a mistake. There's pictures and text messages from her. I loved that girl with everything I had. I was just too young and dumb to handle that strong of emotion.

Mirror Talk

Sitting on the toilet,
chin on my chest,
drifting,
room spinning,
a tear falls.
Weeping starts,
I look up in the mirror,
hating what I see,
why couldn't I get it right?
Why couldn't that be me?
I know why,
I'm f—— stupid.
A degenerate
piece of s——,
dumb twit,
you deserve those tears.
You hurt her,
Young,
Dumb,
immature.
Now she's playing you.
F—— your friends
and you get to watch
his hand
slowly
moving

to
her
crotch.
No…
You deserve that s———.
F——— you.
Tears drown my words,
I bang my head on the counter,
turn around, and throw up,
trying to release the impurities of my soul.
I go to bed sad,
what was supposed to be a sweet night turned sour.

It Doesn't Always Show

It doesn't always show.
There are no cut marks on my wrist,
no burns on my body,
no broken bones in my hand,
I haven't spent any late nights forcing myself to vomit.

I harm myself.
I can feel the harm more.
There's one pain you can't become numb to,
the worst harm you can do to a human is psychological.

I hear the voices in my head
violently reminding me of my inadequacies.
My abuser lives in my head.

He talks to me,
he tells me what I already know,
constantly repeating the monstrosities of my life,
but my trauma doesn't always show.

Happy on the out,
sad on the in,
wanting to die but knowing that I'm not even
good enough for the game to end.

No one asks if I'm okay,
I look just fine.
They have no impression of what goes on in my mind,
and if there's nothing on the outside,

then no one asks.
Ever.

Which means no one ever has to know
about the mental breakdowns
until I pull the trigger.

Just Not Yet

Driving along the winding country road,
flat land stretching across the horizon as far as I can see.
Then there's little old me.

In a land that bears plentiful bounty of wealth and happiness,
I feel so empty.
The world so big,
I, so small.
If I left, it probably wouldn't matter at all.

Would it hurt?
Would I even die?
If I did, where would I go?
Or am I trapped on this earth forever?

Spinning, spinning,
same soul, different body.
Only one way to find out.

I can't do it,
I don't know why,
just not yet…

On the Same Frequency

On the same frequency,
you can't hear but you can see.
Color in the sky sets me free,
everything I want is a possibility.

I see you and I see me,
I see everything we could be.
I see sadness, happiness,
I can see an easy escape from all of this.

I can feel the colors,
kiss trees,
I know all the answers,
and through all of it, I still see you.

On the same frequency,
it's just you and me
rushing through my soul, I can see the breeze
and your entrancing beauty, so powerful it brings me to my knees.

On the same frequency,
you can't hear but you can see.

January 24, 2019

    The dreams I have about her are f—— odd. I don't have time for women right now. Plus, she's happy with her new man. It's been eight, no, nine months. It's time to move on. Just wish my subconscious would knock this s—— off.

February–April 2019

*Deep depression—lost touch with myself and the writing world…
No journaling. The pen saved me. During this time, there was no saving,
just trying to exist in the world. I was lost, severely lost.*

Showtime

Drugs make you happy.
They make me dark.
I sit in an empty room
at a desk that has nothing on it except brooding silence.
I put my face in it,
snort a line of sadness,
try to look like I own nothing but happiness
because that's what I'm supposed to be.

I look in the mirror, and it swallows me,
I smile and now I'm ready.
I look at my clothes, I pop my collar.
I'll return to get some more in the after hours.
I'm ready to party,
not be myself, not say sorry.

I grab my smile and put it on,
I walk through the door,
the lights hit me,
it's showtime for the people;
like a good actor, I'm not me anymore.

April 4, 2019

All I've ever wanted to do was bring light and purity into this world. Hopefully, I can put it into people's souls through the culture I create with my art. I think I've come to terms with living without her. I think about her every day at least once, and she's in my dreams, but the pain in my heart is gone. I'm kind of numb nowadays and I need to find a purpose in the world. I hope my poetry offers help to those struggling with their demons. For me, it's not about being somebody for everyone else but being somebody that I can be proud of. I'm tired of being the golden boy. It's time for me to do my own thing.

Someone There

I don't need a hug.
Sometimes I don't need to talk.
I just need you there.

Creature

I creep up close to it,
what a beautiful creature,
unlike any I could compare it to.
Its beautiful blond mane flows so valiantly down to its shoulders,
broad shoulders and powerful legs made from
a touch of this and a touch of that,
as if god was a meticulous painter.
God created a killing machine.
Its piercing, cold blue eyes look off into the distance,
a creature capable of so much harm,
but it chooses love with a gentleness like no other.
Possibly the most misunderstood creature in all the wild.
So beautiful,
so human,
so...
me.

April 28, 2019

    On days like this, I text one thing: "Anyone wanna get high?" I get ten replies. I guess we're all running away from something.

Teenage Dreams

We were sixteen,
a mystical time full of dreams,
aspirations, and hope.
You offered the most.
You were my queen,
a teenage dream.
Mostly wet,
that was the problem,
so perfect from head to toe.
I loved you for every aspect of your body,
but our minds never connected.
We make up,
Your car, my car,
Your house, never mine.
You were the first and hopefully the last,
but that never had a chance.
I wish I saw it from the start,
I listened to my heart,
that's where you got me.
You kept yourself safe,
sex was just sex,
never love.
Sixteen,
so young,
so vulnerable.
You took my hopes and dreams.
You broke me.

The Greatest Teacher of All

The pain in my heart that causes me to double over
because it twists my soul every which way
until I'm a contorted figure that looks inhuman,
was the greatest teacher I could've asked for.
The pain made me cry,
made me hate my life because I didn't want to
experience such gut-wrenching pain.
It made me the man I am today.
I tried to stand up,
walk back to her for the thousandth time,
but it sat me down.
I hate pain.
Sometimes I fear it,
but pain loves us.
It is the greatest teacher of all.

The Rain Has Changed

I'm stuck in an eternal rain.
I let it drench my every being,
washing the sins and pain away.
I used to be miserable,
but now the rain's beginning to change.

It used to be cold, unpleasant November rain,
the heavy sideways rain that sticks to your skin and never lets go.
It sits on you, eats you,
drenches your clothes, and makes them stick to you.
The kind of rain that makes the urge to take
a warm shower grow tremendously
just so you can escape its blatant harshness.

My outlook has changed,
with it, the rain.
Starting to see the answers
within the rain, I can solve the pain.
This rain is much lighter,
in fact, refreshing,
like the first rain in July after a drought.
I dance in it,
stick my tongue out,
catching little droplets on my tongue like a child.

Like a flower overtaken by the weeds that grow around it,
I am being reborn with the same seeds.
I used to shine bright like a sunflower basking in the light,
now I'll shine bright again.

Tidal Wave

They brought you up around me again,
later they would apologize for doing so,
saying they never meant to bring any bad memories up.
I shrugged them off,
told them it was not the slightest inconvenience to
bring someone up that I have no attraction
towards anymore,
but right now, my heart flutters up towards my throat,
sitting there like a huge bullfrog ready to jump through my eyes.
It was a tidal wave that I wasn't expecting,
something that I haven't felt in a long time
for reasons I can't explain.
Sadness.
Depression.
Anger.
Depression…again.
It's been two years, but sometimes it still returns like a bad dream,
I try to wake up, but it's as real as it seems,
others around won't let me be

May 14, 2019

Sometimes there's just nothing to talk about…

May 17, 2019

It's called drinking the pain away, it helps—for the night, at least. No matter how much I drink, my feelings are still there when I wake up.

Beauty

It burns through me like fire,
runs through me like rain,
so much beauty in the world
but nothing compares.
I look at you and every string in my heart tears.
My heart collapses,
the blood spills over,
filling me with the hurt blood that was trapped inside.
Now this room feels three feet wide.
I'm numb
because you see thirty people and I only see one.
I can't feel a thing,
just the hurt running through my veins
from my toes to my thighs
all the way up to my heart, then it reaches my eyes.
So much beauty in this world,
and I can't appreciate anything…
except you, girl

In the Corner

Never thought dancing on my own would be this bad,
but now I'm sitting in the corner,
watching you kiss him,
and I can't make my legs move to walk out
of the room because I'm so sad.

My heart breaks with every look.
No, every touch
no, every kiss.
It gets worse and worse.

I'm spinning around and around,
right into the ground,
with every second passing,
so am I,
wishing my life away, wanting to die.

Then I wouldn't have to see,
and maybe you would notice me.
Right now, all you see is him.

looking at him with those big, beautiful brown eyes
and all I can do is take it in.
Your arms wrapped around
Him, looking down,

and me
dancing by myself,
waiting on the day you decide to use me again.

Die, B——

I f—— hate your guts. I hope you choke
on your boyfriend's cock and die.
I hope you sit on a toilet and a piranha eats your pussy alive.
I hope you get herpes and carry that s—— for life,
maybe AIDS, and for some reason, they can't save you.
I hope you age quickly and your snatch
dries up like a f—— hayfield.
I hope you get gross ass bunions and they never get healed.

I hope you have three kids that are…
Well, I hope they're healthy.
They shouldn't suffer because their mom's a b——.

I hope you drive home drunk one night and end up in a ditch,
maybe hit a telephone pole, step outside
the car, and blow your feet out.
I know I shouldn't wish anything bad on you,
but you really do deserve everything bad that happens to you.
I ask myself what I saw,
you're an arrogant b—— who thinks she doesn't have any flaws.
I really do hope you're on a rooftop partying and you fall.

Angry Text to My Brother

Hey, Dyl,
you don't ever let me be average man,
I write every night,
I start my business and I make f—— money,
I get so f—— ripped I'm on the cover of *Sports Illustrated*,
I'm so f—— irresistible, damn it.
We gotta get there,
We gotta work to get there.
She is with him, and I'm gonna make that s—— hurt, bro
I'm so f—— hurt, man,
we gotta make that s—— hurt, bro.

Him?

I know we moved on…but him?
For some reason, I can't picture it,
you and him?
You said that would never happen when we were together,
but now you're with him talking about forever.

Does it have to be my best friend?
I know we go at it, but when do I say when?
You win.

I walked in and saw you sitting there.
Next to him? I thought.
Then those soft, gentle lips of yours touched his,
and I shed a tear for every butterfly that flapped
its beautiful wings in his stomach.
Why him?

Out of all the fish in the sea,
you picked the one closest to me,
and he's not even good enough,
not that I am.

So...I ask, why him?
Is the light of our eternal love still dim?
Or are you here to use him?
I'd really like that,
but that can't be true because we're a thing of the past,
and even though my love goes on, yours will never last.

My Good Friend

You make me warm to my core,
strong in the mind,
weak in the heart.
Every time you say hello, you make me smile,
grabbing my heartstrings and playing with them
until tears fall gracefully from my eyes.
I love you,
but you're no good for me.
I know this hurts, but in order for me to move
on, I have to say goodbye to you too.
Your smooth body tasted so good on my lips,
the good times we had together will never be forgotten,
and at least, you can say my friends always liked you.
I'm walking along now,
saving myself from the sadness induced by drinking,
but I might return one day,
when I'm strong enough to remember on
my own and still stand afterwards.
Thank you for encouraging me to sit in sadness,
I needed that.
You're a good friend.

June 5, 2019

Sometimes the best place in the world isn't really a place at all. It's just anywhere everyone else isn't.

June-November, 2019

The upswing. My emotions are still a mess. I can't necessarily explain them but I am beginning to understand the beautiful madness that is me.

Climbing the Mountain

I climbed a mountain and then I fell right back down,
giving you the time of day,
drowning myself in a tortured hell
because I've been afraid of what I can do,
too focused on my past life with you.
I'm picking myself back up and I'm moving on.
I've seen the top before,
such a beautiful sight,
I was almost done.
No matter what you think, you haven't won.
You know better than anyone
I don't ever give up,
I won't stop climbing until I've found a new top.
You like to paint the picture and place the blame,
but there will be nothing you can say when
I find my newfound fame.
I've been waiting for a real long time,
watching you move on while I sit and cry.
Lost but found again like a game of hide-and-seek
I found myself over the heartbreak,
I'm ready to climb again.
When I reach the top, I'm gonna sit there for a bit
because the hardest fights are the sweetest victories.
The ones that beat you up eventually make you happy.

Go Find Them

Looking into the mirror,
not being okay with what you see,
sitting in a pile of self-guilt,
letting it swallow you up until you're no longer you.
Voices in your head telling you to end it,
you hating you for being you.
Look at where you've gotten,
you're even lower than before,
self-hatred gets you nowhere,
it just stands in the way of who you are.

Stands in the way of who you're meant to be,
the son,
the father,
the partner,
the full of life happy lover.
How do I know you were meant to be all this?
Because I am you,
and in order for you to fall this far, you had
to be pretty high at some point.

In this life, you were once on top of the highest mountain,
but you just revealed that there are higher peaks to find.
Go find them.

Moving On

It's hard trying to move on.
The walls around my hearts have now become
the largest fortress in all the land
with the greatest army to protect it,
whoever climbs it will have to be a real hero.
Not some fake hero that says she'll stay
interested but one that actually will.
It's hard putting myself out there,
I've never been real good at this whole talking thing, anyway,
but now it's even harder.
I don't believe anything someone says,
I look for the bullshit in a conversation and I'm at
the point where I can't have the heart break
again because I might break with it this time.
Fear makes a casual conversation, a marriage proposal,
in a time where casual is everything.
I thought losing you was the hardest part
but maybe it's finding someone that isn't you.

F— You

He said the whole thing was a mistake,
begging me for forgiveness,
he valued our friendship.

I told him we'd always be friends.
I'd never let a silly girl come between us,
we've been boys since we were seven.

Next week…

They're back together.

I guess I'm too nice,
or real friendship just doesn't matter.

December 5, 2019

    Sit there with your rich kid happiness. Make fun of me for my failed attempts at love. Do whatever it is that you fuckers do. You will not forget me...

Natural Attraction

It was one night,
a different kind of night.
The stars were out,
and the nature that surrounded us lay beautifully still,
everything as nature was intended for it to be.
It was only right for us to be attracted,
decide together to
lie in our beautiful physicality,
it was only natural.
Like two animals in heat doing what nature intended,
it wasn't her personality
or her heart.
Even the conversation we had before was
not intellectually stimulating,
just physical attraction at its purest form.
I must admit,
it was much relief to me to find a love with no responsibility.
No clinginess,
no gentlemen duty.
There would be no cuddling,
no mandatory breakfast the next morning.
Just us in this moment,
loving recklessly,
choosing each other naturally.

A Truly Beautiful Act

My young mind,
innocent and judgmental,
harsh on those lost souls searching for love in a stranger's bed,
looking down upon them like society upon prostitutes,
I was once too righteous of a person to do such a thing,
listening to Father's propaganda.
Now I realize there's beauty in such an act,
a true stranger taking me in so the pain doesn't hurt as bad tonight.
Talking about our exes in an attempt to heal each other,
a true act of kindness,
two broken souls bonding together
under the moonlight,
skin touching skin,
completely vulnerable for the first time,
and I know I'll be able to finally sleep tonight.
Even though you'll be gone when I wake
up, you care about me right now,
and there's something beautiful about caring in the present.

Final Shot of Love

I saw you at the date party this weekend,
I didn't even know you were in the same sorority.
My friend knew,
he didn't tell me.
He was afraid of what my night might be,
I guess ignorance really is bliss
because when I saw you looking so beautiful
in that flowing dress that complimented your figure so well,
my heart never missed a beat,
my hands stayed dry,
and my mouth stayed perfectly wet.
This was a new feeling,
one that you've never given me for.
It was truly bland in every way.
I saw my other "friend" struggle with you,
growing frustrated as you took your clothes off in front of everyone.
You loved the attention,
you loved that I got none,
but I've always been comfortable in the corner
while you crave center stage.
For the first time since the breakup, you didn't ruin my day
because you were in the game, but I chose not to play.
After that night, I think I can finally say,
I understand now,
and the healing has made the pain go away.

December 10, 2019

Couldn't bring myself down today no matter how hard I tried. My demons may be friends now. I am beginning to float in a heavenly manner on this journey I'm on.

Good Day?

I had a good day today,
I think?
I haven't had one in so long it's hard to tell.
It's like a memory that you think might be a dream but feels so real,
my mind was peaceful,
like it was on vacation from the clouds that
usually hover over my mind.
I had a pocketful of sunshine that I released.
I smiled.
I smiled.
It's been too long since I've felt the corner
of my lips turn up in happiness,
my teeth saw light,
so did my soul,
tomorrow could change everything,
but for now, I'm okay.
I think I actually had a good day today.

Who Is He?

"Fine is boring. You wanna be the man."

The man,
who is *he*?
It seems to me there's pressure to be someone I'm not.
People have always struggled to understand me.
Academia,
athletics,
get a good job,
marry young,
grow old,
be happy in this life *all* the time.
The man does all of these things in perfect grace.
I've attempted to do all these things but I'm not any good at 'em.
My academics make you smile,
my athletic accomplishments line the wall of the school,
proud as can be,
but that's not me.
I'm not sure why I don't check all the boxes,
I just don't.
There's no explanation for
my commitment to art,
my deep reflection on my self-affection,
the occasional sadness swing I tend to take trips on.

I'm not the man,
I'm just me.
Sometimes that falls short, so
I have to ask,
who is *he*?

Emotion's Okay

I'm getting better every day now,
things are starting to come together for me somehow.
As I look to the future,
feelings arise that make me unsure.
I still get scared, frightened, and overwhelmed,
I still put myself in dark places that come
down on me like a guillotine
for reasons that I'm not sure I can make out.
Not because I know and won't but
because I don't have the words to express my
need for a complete range of emotion.
Like a child that needs to dream,
I need to feel,
I am human,
that's what makes me different.
I could spend my days like a mindless robot
programmed to act like I have everything figured
out,
or I can admit that sometimes sitting in my own sadness feels good,
feeling the weight sink down and sit in my stomach,
it's special.
Not knowing what's going to happen to me next
adds a little mystery to this, "Oh so predictable
life."
Being scared is a part of life,
part of growing up,

not knowing to deal with the emotion or push it away.
Unfortunately for most, this decision has already been made.
I still fight with it.
This adolescent struggle may continue on
through life until the days grow long, but
I'm okay with that.
Even though it may seem as though I'm lost,
I'm not afraid of the demons they call emotions.
Emotion might be okay.

I Write For Me

I used to sit at this lonely desk,
looking at the black crows quietly perched outside the window,
and think,
god, give me wings like that bird so I can
get away from this hellish place.
I need a new place with a new heart to give me my new start.
I'd sit there thinking about you,
crying as I wrote for you.
Writing how you were the best thing that ever happened to me,
how you made the trees grow and the birds sing.
Like the sun,
you were the beginning and the end of my day,
but something rose out of the ashes of those deep, dark nights.
I proved to myself that I don't need wings after all.
This pen gives me my escape,
and I may not have control of how you feel about me,
but I do have control of this pen.
So it will no longer write poems of utter despair,
it will sing praises with beautiful phrases of happiness.
Indeed, I've found my wings, and they have set me free
because I no longer write for you anymore…
I write for me.

Reminiscent Technology

It's a self-medicating method to produce a
sense of melancholy in your soul,
offers a sense of memory,
better days were once here,
and they came frequently.
That's where the picture of us in your car once stood,
and that one there is about me too.
Scrolling up,
scrolling down,
freeze frames of the thoughts in that beautiful mind I so cherish.
You only kept the bad thoughts about me, though,
painting me in a light that's not so appealing to the eye.
I know I brought much more shine than this,
so I choose to reminisce on the good, happy thoughts,
the ones that were light like a wedding dress on the big day.
Most people block each other,
remove each other from their hearts and their feeds,
promising to never think or speak of another again,
but they still do.
I won't deny my emotional attachment needs,
I won't feel weak for missing you when I need someone to hold me
or reminiscing on the light thoughts you once held about me.
I'll scroll and
I'll think of
all the things you've taught me.

Thank-You Note

Rummaging through these old dusty drawers,
moments in life in their paper form,
there's the English paper I was once so proud of,
here's a picture of the day I got my first ball glove.
My dad and I, after all these years,
a relationship still filled with love.
Under all the good memories I find one that brings back the bad.
A note
from your mother,
thanking me for taking care of you.
I guess that's what I was,
wasn't I?
A caretaker in a time of confusion and distress,
the firefighter brave enough to take on your burning building.
I put them out but you always found new ones to start.
Our home built with an arsonist inside, it was never meant to last.
To many people this is just a card,
even to you,
it's just a meaningless piece of paper that needs to be
thrown in the trash, never to be seen again.
But to me,
it's the last part of you that I still have,
how I held you,
how I told you I'd never leave,
how I prayed for you, even though I don't believe,
you were my everything.

It's only right that I kept something from
a person who didn't like me.
It's a reminder
I don't belong there
because all I ever did was try and please her.

Just Wanted a Teddy Bear

Maybe the reason why I held on so long is because
you were the only thing I loved about me.
I took you in,
swallowed you up,
me became *we,*
I had no identity.
Like a newborn attached to his mother,
I was not my own person.
When you were happy, so was I,
when you were sad, depression never hit me so bad,
my highs and lows were always too great to handle
because I was dealing with the emotions of
two people.
I broke two hearts,
I broke them apart.
The next day, I had a heart that I didn't recognize.
Although it was damaged and broken in every way,
I cherished it like a hand-me-down teddy
bear.
I patched it up,
duct tape and all,
I dragged that heart with me everywhere I went
until I made it mine.
It might be used, beaten, and torn,
but it's mine and it makes me happy.
I think I held on so long because I wanted your teddy bear,

and you were kind enough to share for a little bit,
but there were rules that I had to abide by,
and I still wanted the teddy,
much like a three-year-old who couldn't
get ice cream after the game.
My hopes and dreams were crushed.
Then my mother found me one,
she helped me find that old, dirty heart of mine,
and we restored it until it felt just fine.

My Path

I may be walking in a different direction,
somewhere far off in the distance where we never meet again,
but I don't think that would've ever happened.
I keep on walking but I can still see you,
no matter how far I get, you're still in my eyes,
once the only star in my dark night sky,
so don't say I ever turned my back on you.
I was always there and still would be,
that's if you wanted me,
even when we weren't together, I stayed,
helped hand you off to the next guy like a dad at a wedding,
I sat and watched.
Scared, afraid,
I shined the light on your path
but couldn't find any for mine,
I wandered like a toddler in the night,
helpless,
afraid.
I made my way out of the woods eventually,
my dad helping me beat the insecurities,
off I went on my path
crawling, walking, skipping.
I taught myself how to play again
like we used to when we were just innocent children,
but I never forgot you.
All it takes is a call,

I need this or that,
I got it handled.
Can we talk?
Of course we can.
You chose not to use me anymore,
I didn't turn my back on you,
I just started walking down my own path.
You chose to forget I was there,
so if I chose to walk in the complete opposite direction,
we would probably meet up somewhere
again,
but I don't think that's going to happen.

I Feel Bad

It hurt
when he said he was going to your place for some "puss,"
talking about it as if it were some business transaction.
I don't know why I still care,
must be some innate instinct wired into me to protect you.
You're more than just puss,
but I can't help you see yourself anymore.
A girl with so much respect,
now masquerading her low self-esteem with
skimpy outfits and drunken offerings.
I care
because I saw your future when I was sixteen,
and it looks much different now that it's here.
I feel bad.
Sorry maybe?
I drowned in my sadness,
recognizing the weight of my emotional situation,
but you push it down like most,
sinking on the inside but telling yourself you're on the rise.
It hurt
when he said those words
because your aura suddenly didn't feel so special.
The place you call home didn't carry the same meaning.
What was once my whole world
has become a mere Saturday night distraction.

Maybe It Was Change

Maybe I wasn't hurt over you after all,
just scared that I was growing up.
You were my worst nightmare out of all the
bad dreams that I had dreamed.
I wasn't just losing you,
I was losing friends,
losing family,
losing my home,
drowning in an overwhelming, adolescent vortex,
spinning me around until I was in a new place,
with new friends,
and even though I still had my home,
the bed I cowered in during the dark nights
was new for ten months of the year.
Is it your home if you only visit on vacation?
We had moving, magical moments of young love.
In the end, that love was a disillusioned mirage
our young brains finally saw true,
but it was still love.
You added to the mess,
never helped it,
and I can look back saying that I was heartbroken,
but the reason I took the dive to being a
degenerate wallowing in his own sadness
happened to be the doing of a young brain
misunderstanding change.

Losing love isn't the scary part,
facing change is.
I was sad that I lost you,
but I was devastated when I realized my protected,
adolescent life that seemed so perfect was
changing.

Did I Lose Her?

If you eventually find peace in their absence,
did you lose them?

Done Running

One-night stand
turned into two,
now I'm running on seven.
A week of my life dedicated to sex with friends,
strangers,
others that stand in between.
Some nights have helped heal,
others were just out of curiosity.
I've been around the block now,
and there're many sights to see,
but I'm ready to choose another home for me.
I've been on the road,
staying in many different places,
luxurious hotels,
all-American town houses,
run-down motels,
but now I need a stable place to call mine.
A good heart
with a good attic to put the things I hold on to,
I'll settle down in this one,
grow old in this one.
I've been running around but now I'm tired,
just give me a sure pillow to lie on.

Write My Own Script

You were the star of my show
and the star of your own.
There was no room for me,
so the spotlight stayed on you and watched you grow.

I faded to the background,
withering in the darkness that the curtains casted upon me,
feeling expendable in my own story.

Not anymore,
I say enough is enough,
I do what I want when I want.
After all, I write the script
because this is my story.

I want my story to be filled with the best love there is,
self-love.

19...Almost 20

19…almost 20.
Into a new decade I'm walking,
and I bring my teenage heart with me.
It's much wiser, like an old man that has seen some things in his life,
much stronger after working through those things,
but it's very much the same heart.
So much potential,
just as it had in its prime.
Fragile,
it must be handled with more care than most.
I understand what's in front of me
and I found a woman,
I love her.
The mirror may not always be my friend,
but I know it's all a game.
It's about how I take care of myself.
I've trusted another woman with this precious possession of mine,
but I won't be as foolish with it this time,
two hearts can stay two hearts and still love each other.
My teenage heart understands that now.
19…almost 20,
my heart has survived somehow.

Goodbye

I've found someone new,
whom I hate saying goodbye to.
When I do, I can feel the small old pieces of my
heart flaking off like leather off an old couch.
This heartbreak is new to me,
a good kind of heartache.
She's revealing a part of me I've never seen before,
it seems as though she's given me a chance at love,
not the type of love that is fleeting
but the love that lasts all night.
Through the ups and downs,
the sickness and health,
'til death do us part,
this love is true this time.
How do I know?
you may ask.
My heart's still young and ignorant at times,
but when she says goodbye, I know there's no doubt she will return,
and when she comes, she'll give me a piece
of my new heart every time.
She's not making me into a new man,
she's allowing me to find the one I truly am.
I wake up and smile
because I'm confident enough to say goodbye to someone I love.
Not the farewell, send-off, never see you again
but the goodbye I'd hoped for,
and she's the one I found it in.

First Heartbreak

It ran through me like a twister,
destroying everything in its way in an instantaneous moment.
Quick,
sharp,
full of unintentional wrath.
The first heartbreak you've given me.

All it took was for you to form your lips the wrong way.
Use them as a sword, tearing
through my heart.

That name turned me to stone.
I built back the blocks of the wall you had begun to tear down.

All love has heartbreak.

Forgive Love

Heartbreak will come.
Love has a way of doing that.
No matter how perfect your person is,
it will come.

Your heart must be forgiving.
Love does not mean anything by it,
it's simply a test love likes to put you through.
No matter how damaged you think you are,
your partner may feel the same.
Love is flawed.
She's still beautiful,
humans are flawed too.

Be forgiving,
be understanding,
love with a damaged heart.

No Judgment

Punch that pillow,
kick that dirt,
scream at no one at all until your lungs give out,
recognize those feelings that don't feel so good and accept them,
bring them in and offer no judgment because they
are beautiful manifestations of your soul.
Sit in them,
let them pass.
Your feelings are not good or bad,
and neither are you for feeling them.
They are human and
you are *beautiful*.

Sadness, I Love You

———————————— ⚜ ————————————

I have a deep affection for sadness,
no judgment,
pure love.
I'm not sure where this love comes from,
an innate appreciation of all that this fine
lady has brought me maybe.
There aren't any words to describe the beauty of sadness.
She's warm,
forgiving,
and the best friend you could ask for.
She tells you what you need to feel, not what you want to feel.
She's fuzzy like a childhood memory.
I feel sad for sadness.
The owners of sadness spend so much time berating
her as if she's a hell-bent slut trying to
destroy their psyche.
She's just here to help,
but no one wants her.
She's a lost soul, just like her owner.
Sadness, you're beautiful.
No judgment,
pure love.
Thank you.

Past Lovers

I know I care when you talk about your past lovers.
A jealous person I've never been,
I tell myself it shouldn't bother my heart,
but when
you bring them up, I can't help but ask
myself what you were thinking.
I guess we all had a love of our life, and I'm sorry you weren't mine,
I want to be yours but I know I wasn't your first,
and that's okay.
Most of this has to do with my own
insecurities that I hold from my first,
it just hurts when I see the memories you hold in your eyes
and the words don't come out easily because you're still hurting.
I understand.
Maybe together we can have love for our life,
wouldn't that be a happy ending?

Not a Decision

We all die.
In many different ways
at many different times,
but it is not your responsibility to decide when
that time comes or how it happens.
Read these words and know
you can struggle with your heart,
with your mind,
but you are so much stronger than you think.
You have to get up,
don't do it for the people that want you to
do it for yourself
because just as this book is,
just as a photo, or a painting,
you are art,
touched by the grace of something much more
beautiful than this life on earth,
and that's special.
Go outside,
bask in the sun,
breathe the fresh air that brings so much peace to your mind.
Your time may come in the future,
but you belong to the present.

The Only You I've Ever Met

"You're the only you that I've ever met."
A compliment I won't ever forget.
The personalization,
the sheer truth of this comment,
turned my mind up on itself,
making me think back to a time where I wasn't myself.
Nights crying,
wishing for death,
instead of living for the future, I was reminiscing on the past.
The future is neither here nor there,
I live in the present.
The biggest disservice to yourself is not
being there when you need you,
drowning yourself out with painkillers,
escaping your needs by ignoring them,
self-medicating on this downward slope, descending into nothing.
It all means nothing
until you decide you mean something.
Deal with your emotions the way you want to,
never apologize for feeling the way you do,
get through the tough times and the dark days,
get back to yourself.
When you do make it back,
you'll be amazed.
Something that you should never forget is,
you're the only you that you've ever met.

December 26, 2019

As I look back on this past year, what a sight I see. I started the year low, waking up hungover and a whore by all means. Now I'm ending it with a beautiful girl that loves me dearly. More importantly, I'm ending it with love in my heart for myself. I've been happy, depression has yet to get the best of me again. For that, I am stronger. I struggled today for the first time in a while, but I still want to wake up tomorrow. That is beautiful. I'm almost done with a poetry collection that I've been writing for a year now. I guess I've actually been working on it since I was sixteen. I'm proud of it, but it's not finished.

December 26, 2019

Just because someone has it "tougher" than you does not justify for anyone, or even yourself, not acknowledging your struggle.

Personal Process

They say there're five steps in the grieving process,
but this isn't a f—— step-by-step process.
There are no magical stairs you can climb in life,
you get sad,
you get happy,
you get scared for a second, and the next you're turning on the light.
It's a back-and-forth game you play with
yourself, and only you can figure it out.
A personal process,
heartbreak is.
Do what's right for you.

December 27, 2019

   Those days still happen. I don't know how to explain it to anyone else. Then again, I don't think emotions were ever meant to be explained.

This Is For

This poem is for the blue-collar factory workers
who sweat all day long to provide for their
family of four.
This is for the teenage girl who feels everything
and nothing at once but can't tell anyone.
This is for the boy who is soft in his father's eyes
because he likes poetry, not cars and football.
This is for the woman who looks at the man she
used to love through eyes full of tears.
This is for the man who can never accept love again
because he let go of the only true love he
had ever known.
This poem is not for the life of the party but for the
person who makes sure the life of the party
gets home.
Your work may go unnoticed, but I promise you it's not for nothing.
Even though we may hide behind the shadows of
idolized figures, it's us who make the world go
round.
It's the policemen and the firefighters,
it's the teachers and the union workers that make us who we are.
It is not the girl on the cover of the magazine,
the CEO of the big company.
It is not the popular girl in school, or even the star quarterback,
it's you…you make the world go round.

So next time you lie in your bed during the waking
hours of the night with tears in your eyes,
feeling as though you can't go on,
remember, you are special.
If you weren't, this poem wouldn't be for you.
This poem is for the daydreamers and the silly idea makers.
This poem is for the ones who dare to dare.
This is for the ones who care.
This poem is a piece of me to you.
This poem is for you, the special you that
no one knows about but you.

Treat Yourself

Take yourself out,
buy you clothes,
tell you how beautiful you are,
because you are, inside and out.
Take care of yourself,
company is an option when you love yourself.

Happiness will suddenly be your best friend,
you'll feel like every day is a win
because loneliness is a choice.
When you deny yourself the love you deserve,
darkness and hate are the only things you serve.

Look in the mirror,
show off a little bit
because you're beautiful and you know it.
Love yourself
and your life
because never in a million years were you meant to be a lowlife.

December 29, 2019

F—— *waking up next to you in bed. I want to wake up in your head.*

December 29, 2019

Kiss her. It'll make you feel better.

Dear Sky

Sky,
how I love to look at you.
No matter the time of day, you never fail to
paint yourself in the most beautiful way.
Your dark hair falling beautifully like the
shooting stars that cross your body.
Your eyes burn brighter than the North Star.
When I'm lost,
I look at you.
When I'm sad,
I look at you.
When I'm happy,
I look at you, Sky.
You are my answer,
within you I find my life's truth.
Your sunrises,
sunsets,
make me feel,
and when they're gone,
I miss them every second they fade away.
I'd like to freeze time with you, Sky.
Bask in your precious company,
appreciate the very fact that every day you
have your ups and downs but
you never leave me.

December 30, 2019

    I'm not the guy to tell you how to handle your emotions. All I know is that sometimes you have to let them out so you can fill yourself with new ones.

December 31, 2019

    We spend more time talking to the person in our head than to any other person. Try liking that person.

Ending Message

Teenage emotion, what a beautiful adventure. It's a confusing time of ups and downs, figuring out who we want to be while also finding love for the first time. We all discover these things sometimes—some hold on to who they are, some lose themselves and create new people. While we're in this s—— show, we receive endless pressure to be the idea of "perfect." We don't understand ourselves just yet, how are we supposed to understand life in its entirety?

I hope this collection helped. If you read this, know that you are never alone. You will have your valleys, some peaks, but mostly valleys. That's okay. The emotions you feel so strongly right now will settle, and out of the whirlwind you will emerge. A beautiful person, so perfectly human.

I can't wait to see a world where we all understand that it's okay to be us. No pressure, no judgment, just pure individuality.

Now that would be a happy ending. Wouldn't it?

Peace, Love, Happiness
lambertlance1@gmail.com

One More Thing

The fact of our emotional lives is that it doesn't end. It may be mellowed by the lack of hormones you produce as you get older, but feelings will always be here. Make them your friend. Sit down with them, chat with them, and then let them go on their way. My story continues, and so does yours...

Playlist for the Heartbroken

1. "Whiskey Lullaby" by Brad Paisley ft. Alison Krauss
2. "Break Up in the End" by Cole Swindell
3. "Fuck Love" by XXXTENTACTION ft. Trippie Redd
4. "Can't Lie" by Ali Gatie
5. "Let Her Go" by Passenger
6. "I Can't Fall In Love without You" by Zara Larsson
7. "Slow Dancing in a Burning Room" by John Mayer
8. "Can I Be Him" by James Arthur
9. "Let It Go" by James Bay
10. "Fire and Rain" by James Taylor
11. "Dancing on My Own" by Calum Scott
12. "Someone You Loved" by Lewis Capaldi
13. "Marvin's Room" by Drake
14. "I Fall Apart" by Post Malone

Playlist for the Up 'n' Comin'

1. "Mr. Blue Sky" by ELO
2. "Father Stretch My Hands Pt. 1" by Kanye West
3. "Transportin'" by Kodak Black
4. "Bird Shit" by Trippie Redd
5. "Medicated" by Wiz Khalifa ft. Chevy Woods and Juicy J
6. "Give It Away" by Red Hot Chili Peppers
7. "Tongue Tied" by Grouplove
8. "No Money" by Galantis
9. "On Top of the World" by Imagine Dragons
10. "Love Myself" by Hailee Steinfeld
11. "Headlines" by Drake
12. "Bitch, Don't Kill My Vibe" by Kendrick Lamar
13. "You Don't Know How It Feels" by Tom Petty
14. "Shotgun" by George Ezra

About the Author

Lance T. Lambert grew up in central Ohio where he has been writing poetry since high school. *All Hearts Break the Same* was a book Lance felt compelled to write and share with people so they could find healing in the pages just as he did. Lance is pursuing a degree in English at Otterbein University in hopes to become a high school English teacher one day. He spends his free time watching his younger siblings play sports and coaching baseball.

All Hearts Break the Same is his first book.

CPSIA information can be obtained
at www.ICGtesting.com
Printed in the USA
LVHW051222031120
670569LV00003B/309